BRANCHING OUT

We all know birds live in trees. But sometimes they have strange companions...

FOX
Most dogs and foxes can't climb trees, but the grey fox can. Its den can be 10 metres above the ground.

This is such a hoot!

FROG
Parachute frogs not only live in trees, they glide from one to another using their webbed feet.

CRAB
The coconut crab is huge (over 1 metre wide) and lives completely on land. It climbs trees to find coconuts.

FISH
The climbing perch can breathe air and climb trees.

GOAT
Goats in Morocco have been known to climb trees that are 10 metres high.

DON'T LOSE YOUR HEAD!

Can you be eaten alive and escape? Yes!

Paul Templer from the UK was swallowed head first by a hippo. Paul said he felt trapped in something slimy and smelt rotten eggs. A friend helped him escape.

Eric Nerhus was swallowed head first by a great white shark and said it was like being trapped in a cave. He escaped after poking the shark in the eye with his free hand.

 A crocodile's bite can be 3,700 psi (pounds per square inch). That's like being inside a CAR CRUSHER.

'I think I touched his taste buds,' said diver James Morrow after being swallowed by an alligator. James' mask and snorkel protected him until he got free.

Paul Rosolie agreed to be eaten by an anaconda as a TV stunt. He wore a special snakeproof suit. The snake only managed to swallow Paul's head, before he called the stunt off.

THIRSTY WORK

How much water do animals need to drink each day?

 ELEPHANT =  **200 litres**
(1 bathful)

 **COW** =  **50 litres**
(a kitchen sink full)

 **PIG** = **6 litres**
(a bucket full)

 HUMAN = **2-3 litres**
(recommended: that's 4-6 regular sized bottles!)

 **NO LITRES**

A fennec fox lives in the desert and can spend its whole life without drinking water.

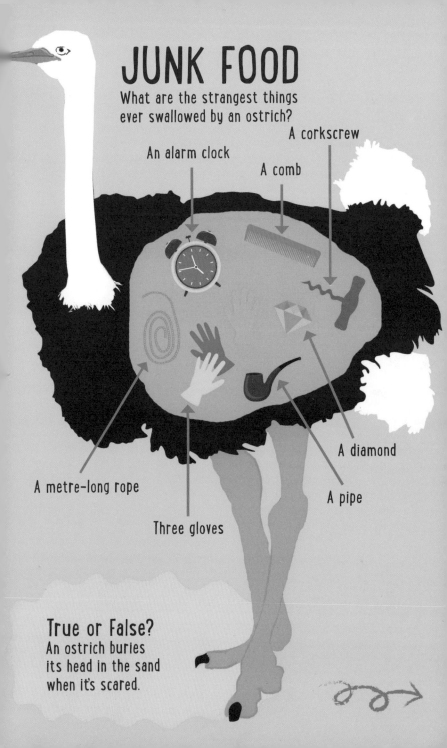

JUNK FOOD
What are the strangest things ever swallowed by an ostrich?

An alarm clock

A corkscrew

A comb

A diamond

A pipe

A metre-long rope

Three gloves

True or False?
An ostrich buries its head in the sand when it's scared.

MASTER BUILDER

Most birds build one nest, but male marsh wrens build an average of 22 nests each year.

Which nest is best?

The female marsh wren picks a favourite – and they move in.

False! When ostriches sense danger, they run away. Reaching speeds of 70 km/h, they are the fastest birds on land.

BARMY BIRDS

Some birds don't bother with nests. Instead they lay their eggs in very strange places.

WHITE TERN: balanced on a tree branch.

GUILLEMOT: perched on a cliff ledge.

The egg is pear-shaped so it doesn't roll off!

TROGON: in a wasp's nest.

The wasps stop predators from eating the eggs

CUCKOO: in another bird's nest.

Massive egg

EMPEROR PENGUIN: balanced on the male penguin's feet.

Doesn't eat for two months

DIKKOP: in a huge pile of hippo poo.

This stinks!

ANIMAL MAGIC

Eye of bat and toe of newt... only witches believe in that stuff, right? Wrong!

Ancient Egyptians would drip bat's blood into their eyes to cure eye infections.

In Elizabethan England, one cure for warts involved chopping a mouse in half and holding it against your skin.

In medieval England, people would eat cat's intestines to cure a throat infection.

In Ancient Greece, owls were baked as a cure for gout (a disease of the joints).

100 years ago in Italy, people ate spiders' webs (and spiders too) as a cure for malaria.

If you were cut by a sword in the Middle ages, you would be treated with a powder made of worms, pigs brains and dead (human) bodies. This mixture would be placed on the SWORD, not the wound!

In medieval England, a sore throat was sometimes treated with dried out dog poo mixed with honey.

Don't try any of these cures. None of them worked!

ANIMALS IN SPACE

There have been 543 human beings in space*, but THOUSANDS of animals. These include:

30 monkeys

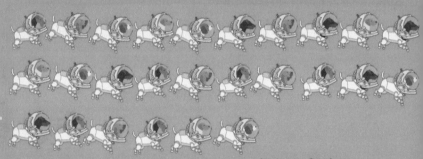

At least 26 dogs

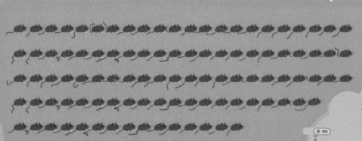

Over 100 mice

Other space animals include:

frogs · cats · geckos · guinea pigs · rabbits · jellyfish

Initially animals were used to test the safety of space equipment, but now they are used for research purposes.

In 2008, 2 spiders spun the first ever spider web in space. Zero gravity meant it was a bit wonky...!

Many of the monkeys went through astronaut training – just like humans! Ham, a chimp who went into space in 1961, helped to steer and control the spaceship.

Animals have broken records well before humans:

1949 – the first monkey in space (Albert II)

 1950 – the first mouse in space

 1951 – the first dogs in space (Dezik and Tsygan)

 1959 – the first rabbit in space (Marfusa)

 1961 – the first human in space (Yuri Gagarin)

NEW BABY

The first space babies were cockroaches, born in 2007. A Russian cockroach called Hope gave birth to 33 baby cockroaches on the Foton-M satellite.

No humans have been born in space... yet.

TOP TRAVELLERS

Roughly how far do animals travel over the course of their lives?

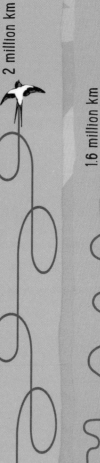

WANDERING ALBATROSS — 6 million km

ARCTIC TERN — 3 million km

SWIFT — 2 million km

GRAY WHALE — 1.6 million km

LEATHERBACK
TURTLE **500,000 km**

DISTANCE TO
THE MOON **384,400 km**

NORTHERN
ELEPHANT SEAL **300,000 km**

HUMAN **120,000 km**

CLAM **0 km**

The Arctic tern migrates from the North Pole to the South Pole and BACK every YEAR. That's a 90,000 km round trip!

You'll walk around 120,000 km in your life. That's about 3 times round the world!

Clams find a place on the ocean floor and then never move again. They can spend over 500 YEARS in one place.

I wandered off the page!

SEA MONSTERS

The biggest animals on the planet all live in the sea.

Giraffe 5m

Human 1.8m

The Portuguese man o'war jellyfish has deadly stingers that can grow to almost 50 METRES.

Pacific octopus 9m

Whale shark 12m

Blue whale 30m

An oarfish can be 15 metres long. Sometimes they like to swim VERTICALLY!

The saltwater crocodile can be 6 metres long. They often swim out to sea to find food.

Ocean sunfish 4m

Giant ocean manta ray 7m (tip to tip)

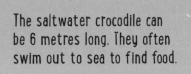

Giant squid 12m

DISGUSTING DINNERS

Some animals eat gruesome grub.

Vampire bats are the only mammals that live exclusively on blood.

Vampire finches peck holes in larger birds and lap up the blood.

BLOOD

There are 2,500 different species of flea. All of them live on blood – and nothing else.

Some leeches get up to 10 TIMES bigger as they drink your blood.

Don't touch the man o'war stingers!

Some dung beetles roll large balls of poo home and eat it there. Others just find a pile of poo and move in!

Rabbits produce a special kind of poo called cecotropes. This poo has vitamins in it that rabbits need to eat to stay healthy.

POO

Gorillas eat their own poo and the poo of other gorillas. Scientists think that this helps them to digest their (other) food.

Ever wondered why poo gets covered in flies? Because they eat it!

Penguins swallow fish and digest them. Then they'll cough up the sicky mixture and spew it into their chick's beak.

SICK

Cows have to chew their food twice to digest it. So they swallow it, break it down, then vomit it back up to chew it again.

One species of moth drinks the tears from elephant's eyes.

TEARS

Some bees sip the water from crocodiles' eyes. This is because tears contain salt and bees need salt in their diet.

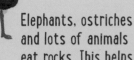

Elephants, ostriches and lots of animals eat rocks. This helps them grind down food in their stomachs.

The bone-eating bearded vulture eats mostly bones. It picks animals up and drops them from a huge height so they shatter into bite-sized pieces!

ROCKS

BONES

ITS OWN BODY

When ribbon worms are really hungry, they eat themselves. They can eat 95% of their bodies without dying. Their body then slowly grows back.

TOILET TROUBLE

It may look like an ordinary toilet, but it can be a HAVEN for wildlife.

A family in India found a 2-metre-cobra in their toilet. It had crept up through sewer pipes.

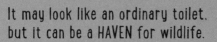

Rats are great swimmers and have been filmed scuttling out of toilets in the UK, US and elsewhere.

There have been several reports of squirrels crawling out of toilets. Nobody knows how or why they end up down there.

Frogs are common visitors in tropical regions. And flushing doesn't get rid of them either! In fact this has been described as a 'frog theme park ride.'

CLOWNING AROUND

Clownfish can control how much they grow.

anemone (where clownfish live)

They live in small groups with a clear chain of command.

Each clownfish stops growing when it is around 80% (or four-fifths) of the size of the next fish up.

The fish in charge is always a female.

If she dies, and the next fish along is a male...

Not only does he start growing bigger...

He also CHANGES HIS SEX and becomes a female!

SPRAY THAT AGAIN

You're stuck on a desert island. You see something squirting water into the air. But what is it?

A blue whale sprays water straight up through a single blowhole. It can reach over 15 metres in height.

A Southern right whale has two blow holes so its spray is V-shaped. Whale spray is a mixture of air, water and snot.

Human
1.8m

A waterspout is a giant column of swirling air and water reaching from the sea to the clouds. It can sink ships and suck fish into the sky. PANIC!

An orca (or killer whale) has a bushy spout. Although they're called killers, they attack seals, fish and birds – not people.

An archer fish is only about 6 centimetres long, but it can shoot a powerful blast of water 3 metres into the air to kill insects as they fly past.

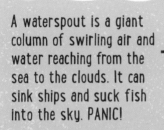

GET MIAOW–T OF HERE!

The Hicks family went on holiday and left their cat Howie with friends in the outback. But Howie went missing...

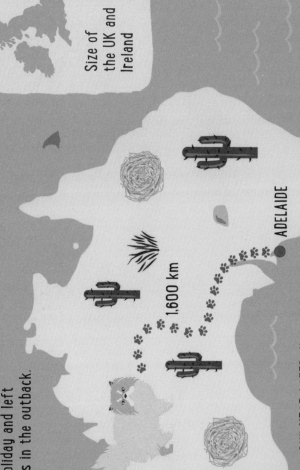

Size of the UK and Ireland

1,600 km

ADELAIDE

ONE YEAR LATER, Howie showed up at the Hicks family home in Adelaide, 1,600 kilometres away.

What makes Howie's trip even more incredible is that Australia contains some of the most DANGEROUS animals on Earth.

SPIDERS!

Australia is home to several venomous spiders, including one of the most dangerous — the Sydney funnel-web. The funnel-web can:

CHARGE at you if disturbed.

STAB you with fangs so sharp they can bite through shoe leather.

CLING ON, biting you again and again.

CAUSE DEATH in 15 minutes, faster than any other spider.

SNAKES!

The 10 most venomous snakes in the world all live in Australia. They include:

The inland taipan, the world's most venomous snake. One drop of its poison can kill 100 men.

The eastern brown snake kills more Australians than any other snake. They are fast and very bad-tempered.

Howie would also have had to face...

dingos   freshwater   scorching heat
                crocodiles   (over 50°C)

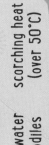

But Howie survived AND found his way home.

LAUGHABLE LAWS

Humans have invented a lot of strange animal laws:

Any whale caught in the UK belongs to the King or Queen.

In Turin, Italy, you have to walk your dogs three times a day.

In Ohio, USA, you're not allowed to dye rabbits.

In Sterling, USA, cats have to wear a tail light when they're out at night.

In Galesburg, USA, it's illegal to keep a smelly dog.

In Chicago, USA, it's against the law to go fishing sitting on a giraffe.

In Baltimore, USA, you can't take a lion to the cinema.

In Switzerland, you're not allowed to own one guinea pig. They have to have a companion.

No horses are allowed in Fountain Inn, South Dakota, unless they're wearing trousers.

Fountain Inn

In Alaska, USA, it's illegal to push a moose out of an aeroplane.

DEAD BUT DEADLY

These animals may look dead. But there's still life in them...

The venom in a stingray's tail still works for a few hours after the animal's death.

The tentacles of a Portuguese man o' war can still sting you days after the jellyfish's death – even if they're not attached to the animal anymore!

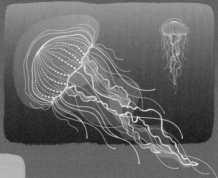

A wasp's venom sac keeps pulsing for a short time after its death – so it can definitely still sting you!

In 2014, a Chinese chef chopped off the head of a cobra to use in a stew. It bit and killed him 20 minutes later!

HOW RUDE!

Humans have given some animals slightly unkind names.

THE WARTY NEWT

THE BLOBFISH

THE STINKBIRD

THE WEEDY SEA DRAGON

THE CRAZY ANT

THE HORROR FROG

The horror frog breaks its own bones to shoot claws through its skin.
Horrible? Or cool?

BEST OF THE BEASTS

Over 50,000 people voted in an Animal Planet poll to choose the World's Favourite Animal. Here are the winners:

Tiger 21%

Dog 20%

Dolphin 13%

Horse
10%

Lion
9%

Snake
8%

Elephant
6%

13% of people chose something else. Is your favourite on the list?

WHO BIT THIS PAGE?

Different critters have different choppers.

DOG

GOOSANDER DUCK
(a duck with teeth!)

huge canine teeth

GIANT AMAZONIAN LEECH
(half a metre long with an 18 cm 'tongue straw')

RAT
(two grooves)

SNAKE

LAMPREY

SHARK

BED BUGS
(several bites in a line)

CAMEL

YOU!
(molars at the back)

THE BOTTOM LINE
Which animal has the best behind?

Fireflies have luminous bottoms. The light can be yellow, green or red. Groups of fireflies can 'flash' their bottom in unison.

Hoopoe chicks defend their nests by shooting a jet of warm poo at any invader.

Sea cucumbers protect themselves by squirting their internal organs out of their bottoms. These organs then grow back.

When disturbed, bombardier beetles shoot a smelly, boiling hot acid out of their butts at lightning speed.

Glass snakes might have the best bottoms. If a predator grabs their tail, it shatters like GLASS. The bits of bottom then jump around, distracting the predator.

FEARSOME PHOBIAS

Which animals are people most scared of?

SNAKES 52% of people

SPIDERS 42% of people

MICE 26% of people

DOGS 14% of people

QUICK QUIZ
There are over 40,000 species of spiders.
But how many species are actually
dangerous to people?

a) 30   b) 109   c) 803

Answer
over here...

Some people have even stranger animal phobias.

Niall Horan of the pop group One Direction is said to be scared of pigeons. Why? 'One flew in through my bathroom window and went for me while I was having a wee,' he says.

Actor Orlando Bloom (Will Turner in Pirates of the Caribbean) is apparently scared of pigs!

Celebrity Tyra Banks is reportedly terrified of dolphins.

Walt Disney, the creator of Mickey Mouse, was said to be scared of mice!

Some animals have phobias too. Ci, a sheepdog from Bath in the UK, is scared of sheep. Instead of him chasing them, they chase HIM.

Do **YOU** have any animal phobias?

CHAIN OF COMMAND

What's the longest food chain you can think of?

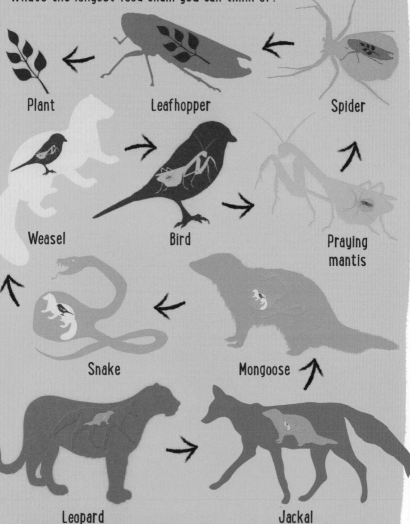

Plant

Leafhopper

Spider

Weasel

Bird

Praying mantis

Snake

Mongoose

Leopard

Jackal

Only 30 species of spider are dangerous to people. No more than 100 people have died from spider bites in the entire twentieth century.

WHAT A BIG BABY!

The paradoxical frog is one of the few animals that gets SMALLER as it gets older.

A paradoxical frog as a tadpole looks like this

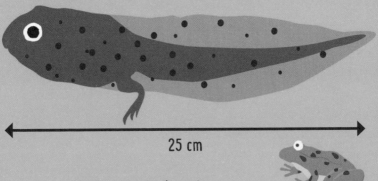

25 cm

A grown-up paradoxical frog looks like this

6 cm

That would be like humans having 7.5 METRE babies that slowly shrank into adults.

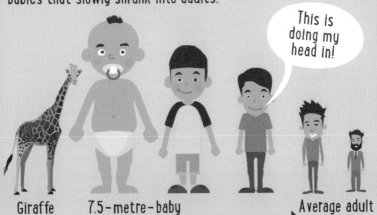

This is doing my head in!

Giraffe
5 m

7.5-metre-baby →

Average adult
1.8 m

SLOWEST MOVERS

How fast would it take different animals to cross this page?

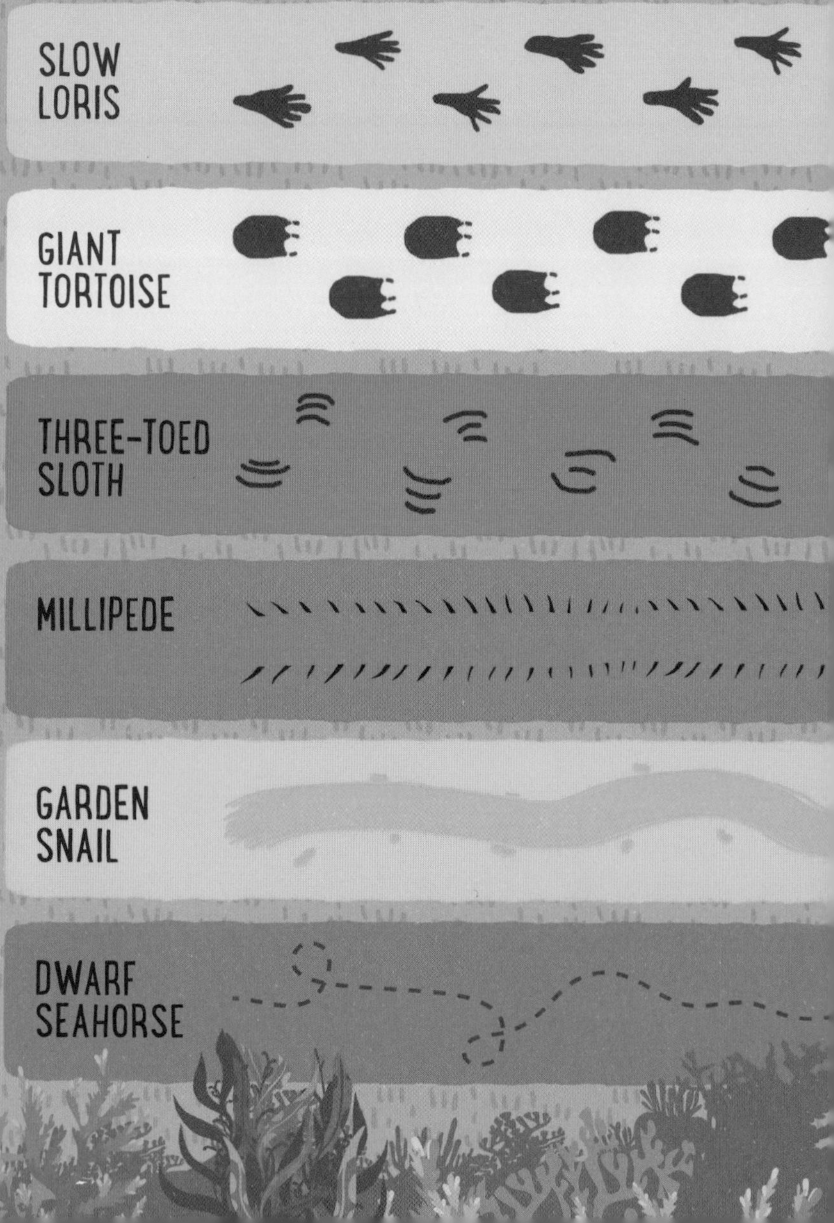

SLOW LORIS

GIANT TORTOISE

THREE-TOED SLOTH

MILLIPEDE

GARDEN SNAIL

DWARF SEAHORSE

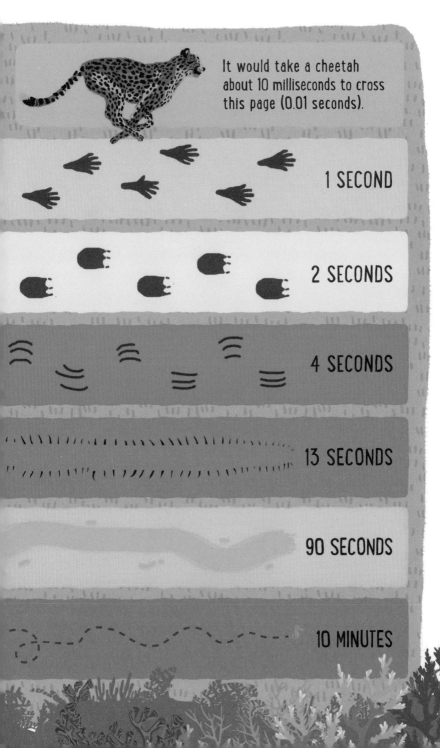

It would take a cheetah about 10 milliseconds to cross this page (0.01 seconds).

1 SECOND

2 SECONDS

4 SECONDS

13 SECONDS

90 SECONDS

10 MINUTES

ANIMAL CRACKERS

What are the barmiest animal stunts?

In 2009, Chinese couple Li Wenham and Yan Hoagie got married, covered in thousands of bees.

They each put a Queen Bee in their pockets and the rest of the hive swarmed them.

In 2009, Ken Edwards of the UK ate 36 live GIANT COCKROACHES in ONE MINUTE.

Australian Tom Buchanan had 125 golden orb spiders placed on his body for 55 seconds. The spiders have a powerful bite – but luckily none of them tucked into Tom!

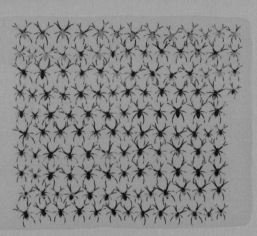

In 2009, Charlie Bell of Leyton, UK, moved 17 kilograms of MAGGOTS with his MOUTH in one hour.

 =

Maggots moved by Charlie Bell = 17kg

Average 4-year-old = 17 kg

WALKING TALL

Which animal do you measure up to?

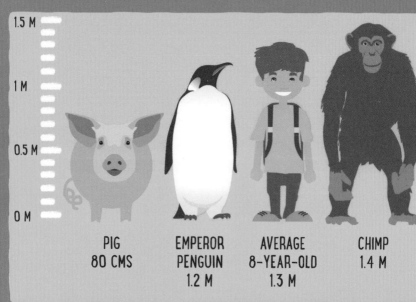

PIG
80 CMS

EMPEROR
PENGUIN
1.2 M

AVERAGE
8-YEAR-OLD
1.3 M

CHIMP
1.4 M

Stick
insect

WORLD'S
BIGGEST INSECT
62 CM

POLAR BEAR
1.3 M

GRIFFON VULTURE
1.1 M

PYGMY HIPPO
1 M

Between the ages of 6 and 12, you'll grow an average of 6-7 centimetres each year.

WALLABY
90 CMS

VELOCIRAPTOR
1 M

GOLIATH HERON
1.5 M

BABY GIRAFFE
1.8 M

World's smallest deer
↓

AVERAGE 10-YEAR-OLD
1.43 M

IMPALA 1.2M
(PLUS UP TO 92 CM HORNS)

MOUSE DEER
35 CM

WALRUS
1.5 M

NATURAL BORN KILLER

Which species is the deadliest?

Every year, sharks kill an average of 6 humans worldwide.

Every year, humans kill an average of 100 MILLION SHARKS.

That was 100 sharks. We'd need another 1 MILLION pages like this to show all the sharks that died last year.

Sharks are mostly killed for shark fin soup, a popular dish in Asia.

In many of these cases, the shark's fin is chopped off and the animal is thrown back into the sea to die.

There are 440 species of sharks, but most never attack people.

Most attacks come from only three species:

Great white

Tiger shark

Bull shark

Some sharks eat ANY OLD JUNK. Here are some of the strangest objects that have been found in sharks' stomachs:

a suit of armour

a set of antlers

a video camera

a porcupine

a cannonball

a whole hen house full of partly digested chickens

FIVE ANIMALS that are way more likely to kill you than a shark:

5 ★ HIPPO: 500 DEATHS A YEAR

If you're in their way, or near their babies, hippos will flatten you!

4 ★ SNAIL: 10,000 DEATHS A YEAR

Freshwater snails live in water that humans drink. They lay eggs containing a deadly parasite.

Sorry...

3 ★ DOG: 25,000 DEATHS A YEAR

When dogs catch rabies, they sometimes bite people, who also catch the deadly disease.

2 ★ HUMAN: 475,000 DEATHS A YEAR

Wars and accidents mean that humans can be a dangerous bunch!

1 ★ MOSQUITO: 750,000 DEATHS A YEAR

Mosquitos carry deadly diseases like malaria. Some scientists say mosquitoes have killed HALF of all the humans that ever lived.

PICK ON SOMEONE YOUR OWN SIZE

Some brave beasties like to tackle
animals much larger than themselves.

The least weasel can take on animals **FIVE TIMES ITS SIZE.**

LEAST WEASEL 40 G   VS   RABBIT 2 KG

With its sharp teeth, it kills by snapping its victim's neck.

A polar bear can take on animals **SIX TIMES ITS SIZE.**

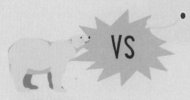

VS

BELUGA WHALE
1,800 KG

POLAR BEAR
300 KG

The bear waits by the whale's breathing holes in the ice.

An eagle can kill animals **15 TIMES ITS SIZE.**

GOLDEN EAGLE
4 KG

VS

YOUNG REINDEER
60 KG

Although it's rare, eagles can carry **CHILDREN** off too. In 1932, a 3-year-old Norwegian girl was carried 1.6 km through the air by an eagle and dropped on a mountain ledge. Luckily, she was rescued unharmed.

A honey badger can beat animals **18 TIMES ITS SIZE.**

VS

HONEY BADGER 12 KG   LION 150 KG

Honey badgers are ferocious and fearless. They have been known to fight off lions and steal their kills.

A wolverine may be the most extraordinary, killing animals up to **30 TIMES ITS SIZE**.

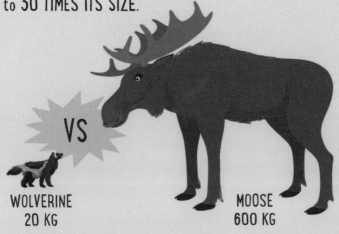

WOLVERINE
20 KG

MOOSE
600 KG

With its powerful jaws and sharp claws, it has also been known to kill polar bears.

The weirdest case of all is the barking spider.

BARKING SPIDER
50G

CHICKEN
2.6 KG

In 1919, one witness saw a barking spider dragging a dead chicken 16 METRES to its hole. A chicken is **52 TIMES** the size of a barking spider.

ONE DIRECTION?

Some animals move in mysterious ways.

CRAB .... SIDEWAYS

MOCHOKID CATFISH .... UPSIDE DOWN

HUMMINGBIRD .... BACKWARDS (often)

SIDEWINDER .... SIDEWAYS

SEA BUTTERFLY .... UPSIDE DOWN

GAZELLE .... ZIGZAG (when escaping)

BASILISK LIZARD .... RUNNING ON WATER

The basilisk lizard has flaps between its toes that stop it sinking. It's sometimes called the Jesus lizard.

There are six animals
hiding on this page...

Turn the page to find
out who they are.

With their white fur (or feathers), these animals are practically invisible in the snow.

ARCTIC HARE

ARCTIC FOX

ARCTIC OWL

POLAR BEAR

ARCTIC ERMINE

BABY HARP SEAL

All of these amazing animals are in BIG trouble.

1979   2016

Because of global warming, the North Pole is now HALF THE SIZE it used to be.

Polar bears and Arctic foxes live and hunt on the ice. No North Pole, no cute animals!

90% of all the world's ice is in the South Pole.

10% everywhere else   90% Antarctica

If all the ice in the South Pole melted, sea levels would rise by around 60 metres.

Statue of Liberty 93 m   Big Ben 96 m   Tower Bridge 65 m   Sydney Opera House 65 m

Want to get involved? Go to wwf.org.uk or www.greenpeace.org.uk to find out more about animals and climate change.

There are four animals
hiding on this page...

Turn the page to find
out who they are.

Nocturnal animals can move, hunt and eat in the PITCH BLACK.

A barn owl can hunt in total darkness. It can hear a mouse's heartbeat from three metres away.

Vampire bats like to hunt on moonless nights – when there is absolutely no light. They use echolocation (bouncing sound waves off their surroundings) to see.

Flying lemurs can glide over 130 metres in total darkness…

…without ever hitting trees – or each other!

Moths use smell to survive at night. A male silk moth can detect ONE MOLECULE of scent from a female silk moth up to THREE KILOMETRES away.

What if humans became nocturnal? How might our bodies adapt?

Tarsier's have enormous eyes (1.6 cm wide) to help them see at night.

If our eyes were like a tarsier's, they'd be 24 centimetres wide.

That's the same size as a basketball.

A bat's hands have adapted to help them fly at night and catch insects.

If human hands were like a bat's, our fingers would be over 2 metres long – and as thin as chopsticks.

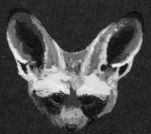

16 cm
Average head width

A bat-eared fox has 13 cm ears and a 56 cm body. Its ears help it to hunt in total darkness.

This would be like humans having 40 CENTIMETRE EARS. Sound strange to you?

Geckos can walk upside down thanks to tiny hairs on their feet acting like magnets.

THE KINGS OF CLING

Which animals are the greatest at defying gravity?

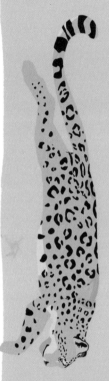

Mountain goats can climb walls and cliffs that are practically vertical.

Snow leopards sprint down vertical slopes, using their claws to cling and tails to balance.

Not only can squirrels climb vertically, but they can fall out of huge trees and land uninjured.

THE GREATEST GLIDERS

Some animals can't fly, but they CAN glide.
Who can float the furthest?

Ouch!

GIANT FLYING
SQUIRREL

hit the edge of the page →

450 METRES

GLIDING
POSSUM

150 METRES

PARADISE TREE
SNAKE

100 METRES

FLYING
LEMUR

70 METRES

WESTERN
FENCE LIZARD

0 METRES

LEAPING LIZARDS!

The Western fence lizard is probably the
worst climber (or best faller). Scientists in
California counted 12,000 falls per hectare
of forest each year. They leap to catch
insects or escape predators... and miss.

WACKY WEATHER
Raining cats and dogs? You ain't seen nothing yet.

In 2009, it rained frogs in Japan.

In 2013, spiders fell from the skies in a Brazilian town.

In Bath, UK, it rained jellyfish in 1894.

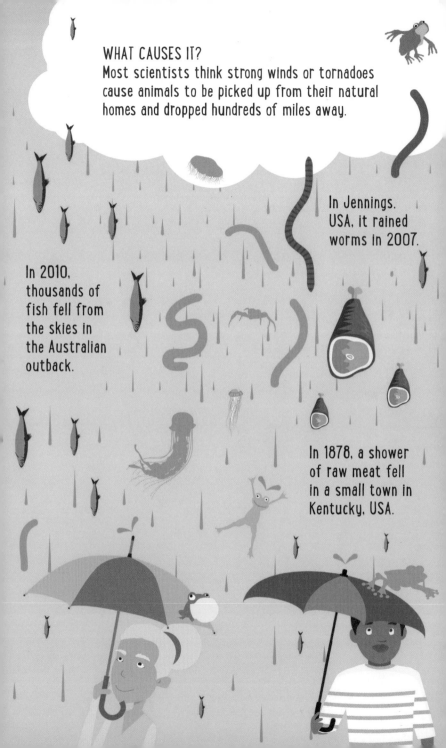

WHAT CAUSES IT?
Most scientists think strong winds or tornadoes cause animals to be picked up from their natural homes and dropped hundreds of miles away.

In Jennings, USA, it rained worms in 2007.

In 2010, thousands of fish fell from the skies in the Australian outback.

In 1878, a shower of raw meat fell in a small town in Kentucky, USA.

ALL OR NOTHING?

Are you a human dustbin or a fussy eater? Animals can be funny about food too.

WHAT DOES EACH ANIMAL EAT?

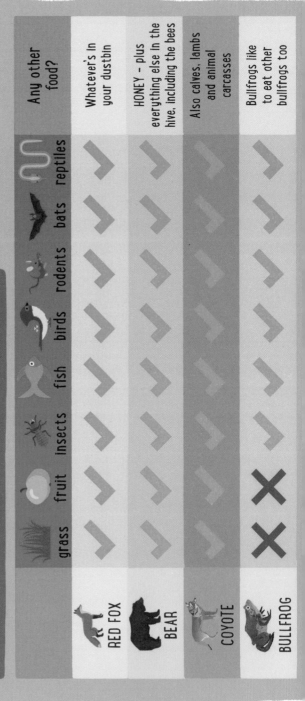

	grass	fruit	insects	fish	birds	rodents	bats	reptiles	Any other food?
RED FOX	✓	✓	✓	✓	✓	✓	✓	✓	Whatever's in your dustbin
BEAR	✓	✓	✓	✓	✓	✓	✓	✓	HONEY – plus everything else in the hive, including the bees
COYOTE	✓	✓	✓	✓	✓	✓	✓	✓	Also calves, lambs and animal carcasses
BULLFROG	✗	✗	✓	✓	✓	✓	✓	✓	Bullfrogs like to eat other bullfrogs too

BIG DIFFERENCES

In humans, males tend to be slightly larger than females.
For animals, it can be very different.

KRØYER'S DEEP SEA ANGLERFISH

Female
120 cm

Male 15cm

The female is 8 times bigger

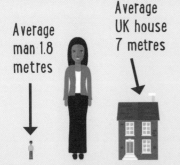

Average
man 1.8
metres

Average
UK house
7 metres

That would be like the average
man having a 14-metre wife.

GIANT GOLDEN ORB SPIDER

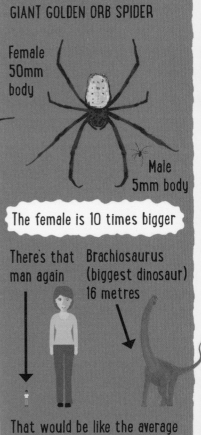

Female
50mm
body

Male
5mm body

The female is 10 times bigger

There's that
man again

Brachiosaurus
(biggest dinosaur)
16 metres

That would be like the average
man having an 18-metre wife.

LETS STICK TOGETHER

After mating, the anglerfish male MERGES with
the female, and they become the same fish.

MINI-MEN

Across the animal kingdom, it's FAR more common for females to be larger. It's only really birds and mammals (like us!) where males tend to be bigger. For most reptiles, amphibians, insects, spiders and worms, women are the biggest!

Male

Female

GREEN SPOON WORM

Female
15 cm

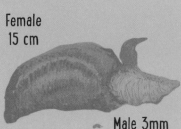

Male 3mm

The female is 50 times bigger

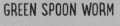

Big Ben 96 metres

Even
smaller
man

That would be like the average man having a 90-metre wife.

BLANKET OCTOPUS

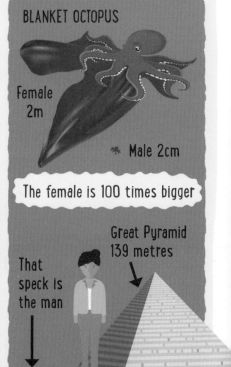

Female
2m

Male 2cm

The female is 100 times bigger

Great Pyramid
139 metres

That
speck is
the man

That would be like a man having a 180-metre wife.

A ROMANTIC DINNER?

Sometimes female spiders EAT the males. This is because the males are small, slow and easier to catch than flies.

PRAWN CRACKERS

The pistol shrimp is perhaps the loudest animal in the world. But how loud are we talking?

50db
human conversation

90db
wolf howling

50   75   100

70db
vacuum cleaner

115db
lion roaring

Bluey, a cat from Cambridge UK, is thought to have the world's loudest miaow. At 93 decibels, that's as loud as a lawnmower.

A blue whale's song is so loud, it can be heard 800 kilometres away.

130db
howler monkey

188db
blue whale's song

150   175   200

160db
human eardrums burst

218db
pistol shrimp's claw

A pistol shrimp's snap is so loud, it briefly makes the water around it hotter than the sun. Any small fish nearby are KILLED by the shock wave.

DID YOU HEAR THAT?

Sometimes the animal kingdom makes strange sounds...

BANG!

In 2005, a python tried to swallow a two-metre alligator in Florida. And exploded.

That was a group of carpenter ants. The worker ants squeeze their stomach muscles and BLOW THEMSELVES UP when intruders approach.

BLAM!

PING!

That was a bullet bouncing off an armadillo shell. It's completely bullet proof.

BURP!

Colobus monkeys say 'Hello!' by doing massive burps in each other's faces.

That was a Texas horned lizard defending itself by squirting blood out of its eyes. Up to a THIRD of its blood can get spurted out.

SPLAT!

HELP!

Parrots can learn up to 800 words.
One of the best phrases to teach them is:
'Help! They've turned me into a parrot!'

FEATHER BRAINED

Some birds build their nests out of twigs.
Others are more... creative.

Crows in Japan have been
spotted building nests
entirely out of coat hangers.

A stork's nest in
the USA contained
17 black stockings
and three old shoes.

This is
cuckoo!

Julie Boaler found
her engagement ring
in a magpie's nest
three years after
the bird stole it
from her bedroom.

Talk about a sticky end!

SPIT AND POLISH
The nest of the edible nest swiftlet is made COMPLETELY OUT OF SPIT. The bird dribbles and dribbles till the nest is 1.5 centimetres deep. When the saliva hardens, the bird moves in.

Gloves, dolls and toy cars have all been found in red kites' nests.

One red kite used TWO DEAD KITTENS as part of its nesting material.

What a birdbrain!

The Galapagos flycatcher has been seen plucking hair from tourists' heads to build its nests.

WORLDWIDE WEBS

Different spiders make different types
of web. How many types have you seen?

ORB WEB

Classic web, great for
catching flying insects.

FUNNEL WEB

A deep funnel with a hungry
spider waiting at one end.

SHEET WEB

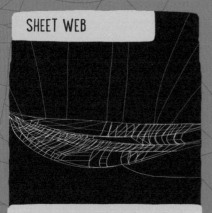

A bit like a hammock. Insects
hit the threads above and fall
on to the sticky sheet.

FLYING WEB

Net-casting spiders throw
their webs through the air
to catch their prey.

TRUE OR FALSE? All spiders make webs.

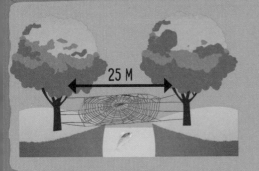

BIGGEST WEB?
Darwin's bark spiders spin webs that can be 25 METRES WIDE, crossing whole rivers. The spiders themselves are only 2 centimetres long.

25 M

The real spider!

WACKIEST WEB?
The cyclosa spider collects leaves, twigs and dead insects and makes a HUGE model of itself in the centre of its web. This is to scare off predators.

A JUMBO WEB?
Spider silk is one of the toughest materials on Earth – stronger than steel. A spider web with strands as thick as your finger could stop a jumbo jet in flight.

WHO'S HANGING OUT UP HERE?
Gossamer spiders have been spotted flying 5 kilometres UP IN THE SKY. They throw out threads of silk and wait for the wind to pick them up.

FOOD FOR THOUGHT

Humans have eaten animals for hundreds of years.
Would you try any of these for dinner?

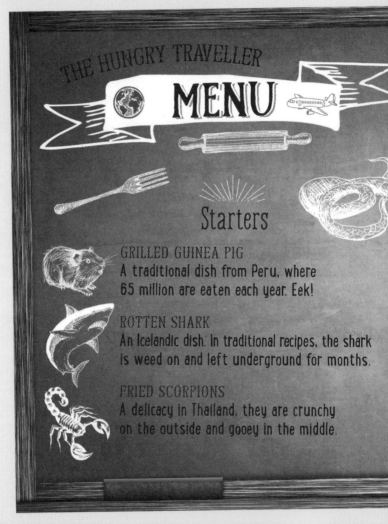

THE HUNGRY TRAVELLER

MENU

Starters

GRILLED GUINEA PIG
A traditional dish from Peru, where
65 million are eaten each year. Eek!

ROTTEN SHARK
An Icelandic dish. In traditional recipes, the shark
is weed on and left underground for months.

FRIED SCORPIONS
A delicacy in Thailand, they are crunchy
on the outside and gooey in the middle.

 FALSE! About half of spider species are
hunters and don't build webs at all.

Jiang Musheng from China has lived on live mice, rats and tree frogs for the last 40 years. He once ate 20 live mice in a single day!

Main courses

LIVE COBRA HEART
A Vietnamese speciality. The snake is sliced open and the heart is eaten while it is still beating. Sssscary!

DRIED STARFISH
Popular in China, you crack off a leg and eat the green mush inside.

Dessert

ROTTEN CHEESE
Cazu marzu cheese from Sardinia is full of maggots. Some people pick the maggots out, others eat them.

WASP CRACKERS
A Japanese creation. It's a big biscuit full of (hopefully dead) wasps.

HEAD HUNTER

Lots of animals are predators. But which is the most successful hunter?

BENGAL TIGER

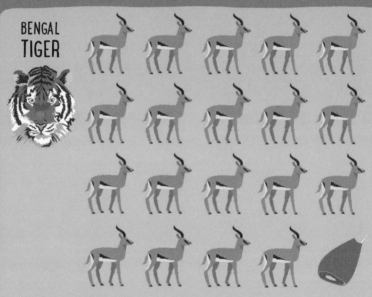

Only 5% of hunts end in a kill.

AFRICAN WILD DOG

They catch their prey around 20% of the time.

GREAT WHITE SHARK

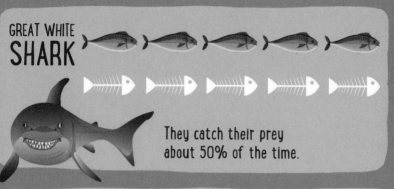

They catch their prey about 50% of the time.

CHEETAH

They also catch their prey about 50% of the time.

DRAGONFLY

Their prey almost NEVER escape – 95% of hunts are successful.

WHY?

Dragonflies are TOP HUNTERS. They can fly forwards, backwards, sideways and upside down. They also have AMAZING BRAINS that can predict where their prey will fly.

DON'T CALL ME THAT!

Do you like your name? Some animals
have names that don't suit them at all.

A killer whale isn't
a whale.

I'm a dolphin,
don't you know.

A black rhino isn't black and
a white rhino isn't white.

Look at us!
We're grey!

Koala bears are
marsupials, not bears.

I can't bear
being called
a bear.

A flying lemur isn't a
lemur and can't fly.

I call it
falling with
style.

PLUS… A prairie dog isn't a dog. A meerkat isn't a cat.

Bird-eating spiders hardly ever eat birds.

I prefer a nice cockroach.

A bald eagle isn't bald. Not even a bit.

Feathers.

More feathers.

A bearcat isn't a bear or a cat.

I'm a kind of civet, really.

A starfish isn't a fish. Nor is a jellyfish.

We're spineless.

And brainless.

Dragonflies, butterflies and fireflies... aren't flies.

Flies have two wings.

We have four!

And I'm a beetle!

And a mudpuppy is definitely not a puppy.

I'm a salamander. Sorry.

A mongoose isn't a goose.

TOP DOGS

Is Man's Best Friend yours too?

THE WORLD'S MOST POPULAR BREEDS*

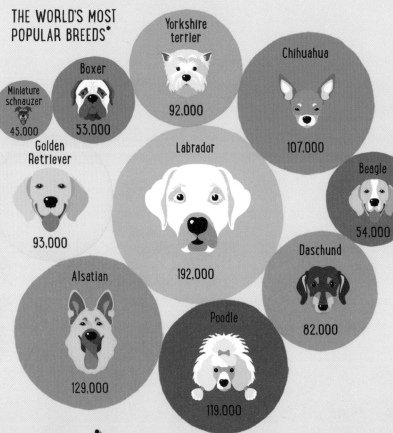

Yorkshire terrier 92,000

Chihuahua 107,000

Boxer 53,000

Miniature schnauzer 45,000

Labrador 192,000

Golden Retriever 93,000

Beagle 54,000

Daschund 82,000

Alsatian 129,000

Poodle 119,000

Although the most popular type of dog is not a breed at all. Around 53% are mongrels – a mixture of breeds!

*(FCI Worldwide Figures 2013 – number of dogs).

A mountain chicken is a frog. A tarantula hawk is

TOP DOG NAMES

UK

Boys

Charlie

Oscar

Alfie

Girls

Bella

Poppy

Molly

US

Boys

Buddy

Max

Jake

Girls

Molly

Daisy

Maggie

THE BIGGEST AND THE SMALLEST

Zeus
World's biggest dog ever

112CM
(paw to
shoulder)

Milly
World's
smallest
living dog

9.7CM

a wasp. A guinea pig isn't a pig or from Guinea.

COOL CATS
Is your cat a purr-fect pet?

What do cats do all day?

NOTHING
(sitting or
sleeping)

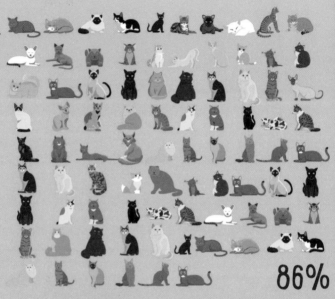

86%

**WALKING
AROUND**

10%

**OTHER
STUFF***

4%

*hunting, eating, playing, digging, going to the toilet, fighting other cats, having kittens

A red panda isn't a panda, and a honey badger isn't

CLEO-CATRA!
Ancient Egyptians thought cats were SACRED.

During one battle, it was said that the Persian army carried cats into battle, knowing the Egyptians wouldn't fire any arrows in case they hit the cats.

This is a cat-astrophe!

NINE LIVES?
In 2012, a cat called Tabitha survived a ONE HOUR 45 MINUTE wash in a washing machine.

(She was lucky to survive. Most cats would have drowned – dont try this!)

I'm one soggy moggy.

FAT CAT?
In 2011, Maria Assunta died and left her $13 million fortune to her cat, Tommaso.

$13 MILLION = 20 MILLION TINS OF CATFOOD

a badger – and doesn't like honey (it prefers the beeswax).

HOW LONG HAVE I GOT?

There are lots of venomous animals in the world.
But which ones kill you the quickest?

You've got
**LESS THAN FIVE
MINUTES** left

You've got
about **THIRTY
MINUTES** left

BOX JELLYFISH
Its three-metre tentacles
contain the world's most
vicious venom! Can kill
you in MINUTES.

BLUE-RINGED OCTOPUS
It's the size of your hand
but contains enough
venom to kill 26 adults.

POISON DART FROG
You'll CROAK if you
swallow just one drop
of this frog's poison.
There's no antidote either.

KING COBRA
A king cobra can kill you
in less than half an hour,
releasing more venom than
almost any other snake.

TRUE OR FALSE?

If a venomous snake accidentally bites itself, it DIES!

You've got **BETWEEN THIRTY MINUTES and TWO HOURS** left

You've got **ABOUT SIX HOURS** left

STONEFISH
Step on one of these and you'll get a deadly spike in your foot. Then you'll have six hours to hop to the hospital.

INLAND TAIPAN
You're 100% guaranteed to die in 45 minutes unless you find an antidote.

BRAZILIAN WANDERING SPIDER
First you'll swell up, then you'll be paralysed then – about two hours later – you'll stop breathing. Yikes!

BLACK FAT-TAILED SCORPION
Ouch! This scorpion has a hugely painful sting. Scuttle off to the doctors within five or six hours – and you'll survive (probably).

MEGABEASTS

Some animals used to be a lot bigger...

Used to be
TWICE
AS BIG

HUMAN
1.8M

RED KANGAROO
TODAY 1.5M

GIANT KANGAROO
3M

Giant kangaroos died out 50,000 years ago.

Used to be
THREE
TIMES
BIGGER

BEAVER
85CM LONG

GIANT BEAVER
2.5 M

Giant beavers became extinct 10,000 years ago.

 FALSE! Snakes tend to be immune to their own venom.

Used to be
**TEN
TIMES
BIGGER**

HUMAN
1.8M

MODERN SLOTH
60CM LONG

GIANT SLOTH
6M LONG, 2.5M TALL

Giant sloths (Megatherium) died out 11,000 years ago.

Used to be
**FIFTEEN
TIMES
BIGGER**

AVERAGE
DRAGONFLY TODAY
5CM WINGSPAN

GIANT DRAGONFLY
75CM WINGSPAN

Giant dragonflies became extinct 300 million years ago

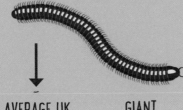

Used to be
**OVER
100
TIMES
BIGGER**

HUMAN
1.8M

AVERAGE UK
MILLIPEDE
TODAY 20MM

GIANT
MILLIPEDE
2.3M

Giant millipedes died out 300 million years ago.

THIS IS THE LIFE!

How long do different animals live?

The male acarophenax mite lives for MINUS ONE DAY. They hatch inside their mother, mate with the females, then DIE BEFORE THEY'RE EVEN BORN!

0 YEARS

RABBIT
3 YEARS

KANGAROO
10 YEARS

TIGER
12 YEARS

RATTLESNAKE
15 YEARS

CHIMP 40 YEARS

GRIZZLY
BEAR
25 YEARS

HORSE
30 YEARS

'CREME PUFF' (OLDEST
CAT EVER) 38 YEARS

GIANT CATFISH
60 YEARS

COCKATOO
65 YEARS

ALLIGATOR
50 YEARS

AFRICAN
ELEPHANT
70 YEARS

BOX TURTLE
110 YEARS

HUMANS
70-80 YEARS

DIPLODOCUS
100 YEARS (ESTIMATED)

GREENLAND SHARK
270 YEARS

GIANT
TORTOISE
120 YEARS

BLUE WHALE
85 YEARS

OWL PARROT
90 YEARS

The turritopsis dohrnii LIVES FOREVER.
When they get old, they
turn back into adults,
then babies. Then their
lives start again!

STAR PERFORMERS?

Do you share a star sign with any of your friends?
Well, some animals ALL have the same sign.

POLAR BEAR

Polar bears are nearly ALL Sagittarians – born in November and December.

It's said that Sagittarians are 'fond of travel'. Well, polar bears can swim for over 400 MILES without stopping. That's a lot of travel!

Scorpio
Oct 23–Nov 21

♏

Sagittarius
Nov 22–Dec 21

♐

Capricorn
Dec 22–Jan 19

♑

CHRISTMAS ISLAND CRAB

Christmas Island crabs are all born at the same time (usually October and November) AND in the same place (Christmas Island!)

Scorpios are said to be 'fierce and independent', and this certainly suits this large, tough crab.

BLACK BEAR

Black bears are usually born in January.

As Capricorns, they are meant to be 'headstrong and determined'. Well, they can smell food from 20 MILES AWAY and will cross roads, rivers and mountains to get to it. Pretty determined!

HARP SEAL

Harp seals are born from late February to mid-March, making them Pisceans.

Pisces is the sign of the fish and harp seals certainly love fish – they eat up to 9kg of them every day.

SHEEP

A high percentage of lambs are born in early Spring, making many of them Ariens.

Aries is the sign of the ram (a male sheep) so this suits them perfectly!

Aquarius
Jan 20-Feb 18

≈

Pisces
Feb 19-Mar 20

♓

Aries
Mar 21-April 19

♈

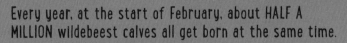

WILDEBEEST

Every year, at the start of February, about HALF A MILLION wildebeest calves all get born at the same time.

This makes all wildebeest Aquarians.
Aquarians are meant to be friendly and sociable, which is just as well as they travel everywhere in a giant migrating herd of 1.5 MILLION other wildebeests.

WOLF

Wolf cubs are born in late April or early May, making then Taureans.

Taureans are said to be stubborn and it's true that once wolves spot their prey, they will chase it all day and night, never giving up.

REINDEER

Reindeer calves are usually born in May or June, making them Geminis.

Geminis are meant be 'energetic and restless' and reindeer are definitely that, travelling over 2,500 KILOMETRES a year in huge herds.

Taurus
April 20–May 20
♉

Gemini
May 21–June 20
♊

Cancer
June 21–July 22
♋

BAT

Bats – in the UK at least – are born in late June and early July.

Cancers are fond of their families and bats certainly like to live all snuggled together. For example, Bracken Cave in Texas, U.S. has 20 MILLION bats living in it. It takes TWO HOURS for them all to leave for their evening hunt.

SOUTHERN RIGHT WHALE

Southern right whales are usually Leos, born in July and August.

Leos are 'brave, friendly but sometimes big-headed'. This suits right whales who are – literally – big-headed. Their head is a third of their body length! This is like you having a head the size of a beach ball!

PANDA

Baby pandas are usually Virgos.

Virgos are said to be 'modest, intelligent but also fussy'. Given that pandas spend 16 HOURS a day eating NOTHING BUT BAMBOO, they can definitely be called fussy!

Leo
July 23–Aug 22

♌

Virgo
Aug 23–Sept 22

♍

Libra
Sept 23–Oct 22

♎

Which animal do you share a star sign with?

HUMANS

The most common time of year to be born in the UK is late September and early October, making Libra the most popular star sign by far. (In the US, it's slightly earlier – the beginning of September).

Librans are meant to be kind and patient. Are you a Libran? Does that sound like you?

EGGS-TRAORDINARY!

Eggs come in all shapes and sizes.

CHICKEN EGG
55MM

blue and
luminous

TINAMOU EGG
50MM

FOREST COBRA
EGG 60MM

GREAT STAR
OF AFRICA
(largest ever
cut diamond)
59MM

PING-PONG BALL
50MM

SEA TURTLE EGG
50MM

VERVAIN
HUMMINGBIRD EGG 10MM

5 PENCE PIECE
18MM

HYPSELOSAURUS
(biggest dinosaur egg)
300MM

WORLD'S BIGGEST
EASTER EGG
8.5 METRES

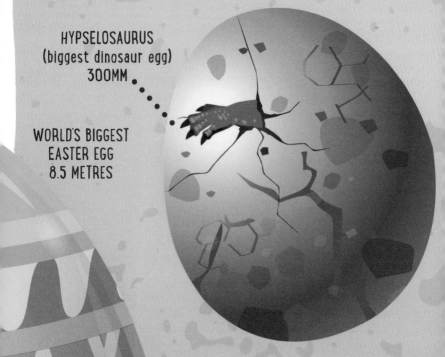

The real-life eggs are exactly THREE TIMES larger than the ones drawn here.

I'm egg-stinct!

PLATYPUS EGG 18MM

TENNIS BALL 66MM

If laid in the sun, the baby becomes male; if laid in the shade, the baby becomes female

CROCODILE EGG 60MM

GIANT WATER BUG 100 MM LONG (male carries up to 100 eggs on his back)

ELEPHANT BIRD EGG 300MM (this three-metre bird died out 300 years ago)

BULLHEAD SHARK EGG 110MM

KIWI EGG 120MM

OSTRICH EGG 180MM

THE HIGHS AND LOWS

Who lives the furthest up? And the lowest down?

An eagle can spot a rabbit on the ground from 3.2km up in the air.

Himalayan jumping spider (highest living land animal) 6.7km

Griffon vulture (highest flying bird) 11km

A colony of bumblebees was found on the slopes of Everest 5.5km above ground.

More than 4,000 people have reached the top of Everest.

Mount Everest 8.8km

12 km

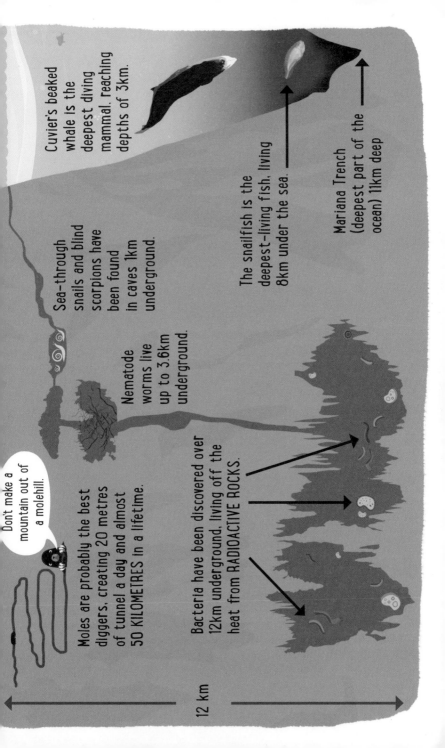

HEART TO HEART

Animals' hearts beat at different rates.

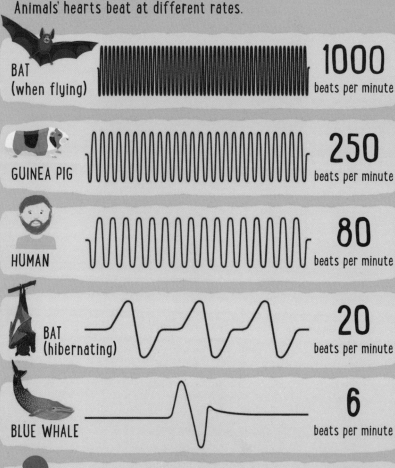

BAT (when flying) — **1000** beats per minute

GUINEA PIG — **250** beats per minute

HUMAN — **80** beats per minute

BAT (hibernating) — **20** beats per minute

BLUE WHALE — **6** beats per minute

JELLYFISH — **0** beats per minute

Jellyfish don't have a heart. Or blood. Or lungs. Or bones. Or a brain.

Or eyes. Or a nose. Or a face!

WAIT FOR IT...

Some animals use 'startle coloration' to scare off animals when they get too close...

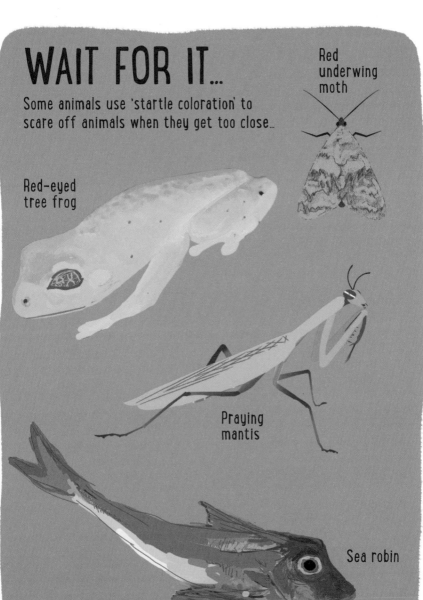

Red underwing moth

Red-eyed tree frog

Praying mantis

Sea robin

These are their normal colours. Turn the page for the **SCARY** versions.

ANIMAL SPEED LIMITS

What is the maximum speed (in mph) an animal can achieve?

28 HUMAN (the runner Usain Bolt)

30 KANGAROO

55 ANTELOPE

70  SAILFISH

75 CHEETAH

200 FALCON (when diving)

25,000 HUMAN (in a rocket)

MIGHTY MITE
The fastest animal, relative to its size, is the Paratarsotomus Macropalpis mite. It can run 322 body lengths a second. That's like you running 1,300 miles per hour!

BOO!

Flashing predators with bright colours can give you precious seconds to escape.

Red underwing moth

Red-eyed tree frog

Praying mantis

Sea robin

 Turn back to see the animals at rest...

TOO MANY OR TOO FEW

In many places, the number of animals is 'just right'
But sometimes human actions can put nature seriously
out of balance.

TOO MANY

LIONFISH   CANE TOAD   EUROPEAN STARLING   GYPSY MOTH

KILLER BEE   ASIAN CARP   ARGENTINE ANT   COTTON WHITEFLY

LOADS OF TOADS

Cane toads were introduced
to Australia in 1935 to contain
beetles that were eating crops.

Now there are over a BILLION
of them.

They are huge, poisonous and
eat everything, including pet
food, which they steal from
bowls outside people's houses.

PLENTY MORE FISH...

In the 1970s, there were no
lionfish in the Caribbean Sea.

Now there are up to 1,000 per
acre, probably because of six
that escaped from an aquarium.

Lionfish lay a million eggs per
year and can eat 40 fish an hour.

There are so many lionfish that
they have started to eat each other!

There are just 57 Amur leopards left in the wild. There used to be thousands.

TOO FEW

ORANGUTAN

JAVAN RHINO

AMUR LEOPARD

CHATHAM ISLAND ROBIN

VAQUITA

TIGER

HAWKSBILL TURTLE

MOUNTAIN GORILLA

BAD MEDICINE

There are around 60 Javan rhinos left in the world.

Rhinos are killed by humans for their horns, which are used in traditional Chinese medicine. This medicine doesn't work!

Rhino horns are made of keratin, the same stuff you hair and nails are made of. So it's like trying to cure a disease by eating your toenails!

FLYING HIGH

Humans can help to put things right too.

In 1980, there were just FIVE Chatham Island robins left. A conservation programme was set up and now there are around 300.

Find out how YOU can help at wwf.org

DO YOU SQUEAK RAT?

Rats wee all over the place – and on each other.
That's because they use their wee to communicate
information about their age, mood and more.

RAT
PHRASEBOOK

I'm 3 years old.

I've just been in a fight.

I'm a brown rat, not a black rat.

I'm the leader of this pack.

I'm in a good mood
at the moment.

This food is delicious.
Try some!

WHY DO RATS WEE ON THEIR FOOD?
Rats can't vomit so they have to be careful about what
they eat. Weeing on food is their way of saying: 'This is
safe. It might taste a bit wee-y now, but you can eat this'.

WEE WINNERS

Which animals have the weirdest wee?

THE MOST WEE?
Fin whales produce about 970 litres of wee every day.
That's enough to fill five bathtubs.

Humans produce
about a litre and
a half each day.

1 LITRE 0.5 LITRE

THE BRIGHTEST WEE?
Cat wee GLOWS under
ultraviolet light.
Mouse, rat (and human)
wee glows a little too,
but cat wee is considered
the brightest.

SHOWERS

THE MOST SPECIAL?
The Mundari tribe in South
Sudan love their cows.
Every morning, they stick their
heads under their favourite
cow – and get weed on!
The cow wee gradually
turns their hair orange.
But it also stops infection
and kills bacteria!

TIME TO GO!

Some animals poo a lot, some animals poo a little.

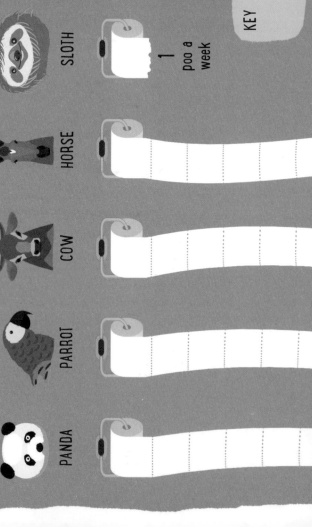

PANDA

PARROT

COW

HORSE

SLOTH
1 poo a week

HIBERNATING BEAR
No poos for 7 MONTHS!

DEMODEX MITE
NO POOS EVER!

KEY

1 sheet = 1 poo a day

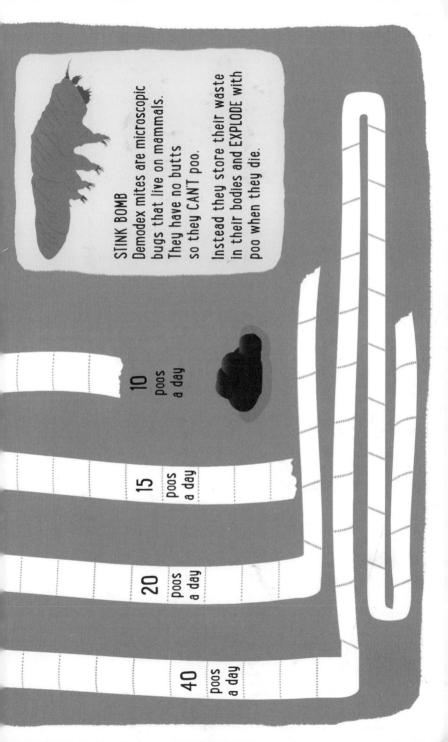

STINK BOMB
Demodex mites are microscopic bugs that live on mammals. They have no butts so they CAN'T poo.

Instead they store their waste in their bodies and EXPLODE with poo when they die.

10
poos
a day

15
poos
a day

20
poos
a day

40
poos
a day

SOURCES

This book wouldn't have been possible without a huge number of AWESOME animal books and websites. Here are just a few of my favourites:

BRILLIANT BOOKS:
Extreme Nature by Mark Carwardine (Collins, 2007)
Guinness World Records 2017 (Guinness Publishing, 2016)
How Much Poo Does an Elephant Do? by Mitchell Symons (Red Fox, 2009)
How to Avoid a Wombats' Bum by Mitchell Symons (Red Fox, 2008)
It Can't Be True! (Dorling Kindersley, 2013)
National Geographic Kids Infopedia 2017 (National Geographic Kids, 2016)
Strange But True! (Dorling Kindersley, 2015)
Supernature by Derek Harvey (DK Nature, 2012)
The Book of Animal Records by Mark Carwardine (Natural History Museum Press, 2013)
The Horrible Science series by Nick Arnold (Scholastic, 1996-2009)
The QI Book of Animal Ignorance by John Mitchinson and John Lloyd (Faber and Faber, 2015)

WONDERFUL WEBSITES:
BBC Earth: http://www.bbc.com/earth/uk
Encyclopedia Britannica: http://www.britannica.com
National Geographic Kids: www.ngkids.co.uk
National Geographic News: http://news.nationalgeographic.com/
The QI Elves on Twitter

Newspaper websites to look up:
The Guardian, The Telegraph, the BBC and The Daily Mail.

And, of course, Google.
For a full list of ALL the books and sources I used, go to: https://goo.gl/2968e9